Welcome

A spool of thin shiny wire, sparkly beads, and a metal crochet hook are all you'll need to create unique elegant jewelry to accessorize your wardrobe — just like the expensive pieces found in high-end boutiques. See how easy it is to use simple crochet stitches to fashion wire and beads into glamorous necklaces, bracelets, belts, or fanciful flower pins. Fill your jewelry box with eye-catching creations that will spice up all of your ensembles with pizzazz. Crocheting with wire will quickly become a fun and meditative craft where the possibilities are endless. You'll feel a bit like a wire sculptor as you create these projects or use the techniques to jump-start your own crocheted jewelry designs.

About Basha

Drawing upon her background in advertising, art direction, and graphic design, Basha Kooler is an accomplished craft designer, writer, and photo stylist for Kooler Design Studio. Besides utilizing her talents for styling the beautiful photographs in KDS books, Basha has also written several craft and home décor books and contributed projects and designs to a variety of other KDS titles. In addition to her many creative interests, Basha loves hiking and spending time with her 11 year old daughter Thea.

contents

wire & bead basics

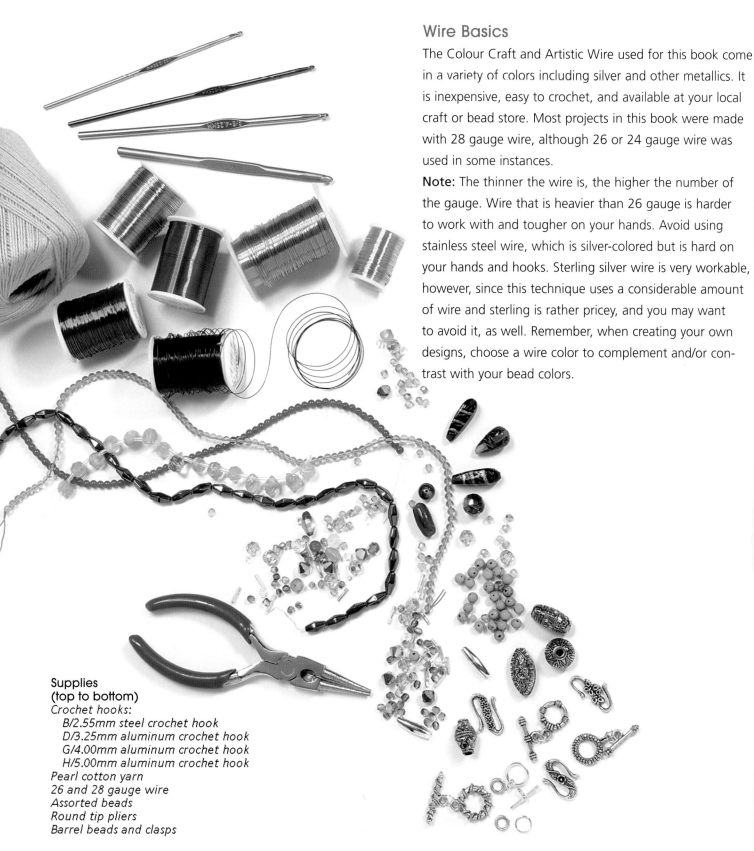

Wire Basics

The Colour Craft and Artistic Wire used for this book come in a variety of colors including silver and other metallics. It is inexpensive, easy to crochet, and available at your local craft or bead store. Most projects in this book were made with 28 gauge wire, although 26 or 24 gauge wire was used in some instances.

Note: The thinner the wire is, the higher the number of the gauge. Wire that is heavier than 26 gauge is harder to work with and tougher on your hands. Avoid using stainless steel wire, which is silver-colored but is hard on your hands and hooks. Sterling silver wire is very workable, however, since this technique uses a considerable amount of wire and sterling is rather pricey, and you may want to avoid it, as well. Remember, when creating your own designs, choose a wire color to complement and/or contrast with your bead colors.

Supplies
(top to bottom)
Crochet hooks:
  B/2.55mm steel crochet hook
  D/3.25mm aluminum crochet hook
  G/4.00mm aluminum crochet hook
  H/5.00mm aluminum crochet hook
Pearl cotton yarn
26 and 28 gauge wire
Assorted beads
Round tip pliers
Barrel beads and clasps

Before starting a project, crochet some chains with wire until you get a feel for the hooking rhythm and correct wire tension. Start with the most inexpensive thin wire you can find and a large crochet hook. Practice making a chain and then single crochet row after row to create a uniform look.

It takes a little practice to feel comfortable crocheting with wire, keeping the loops loose and flexible so the hook can move freely through the loops. Pulling the wire too tight will cause frustration. However, to its advantage, unlike yarn, wire is very forgiving in that it is easy to "fudge"— you may add a stitch or drop a stitch wherever needed, and it will not be noticeable. Stretch or pull the wire fabric to block it and manipulate it into the shape and form you desire. The perfect pattern of row after row is less important than the final "shape" when using wire. It is practically impossible to unravel wire more than a stitch or two, so just keep going and incorporate your mishaps into the design.

Bead Basics

Due to the current popularity of beads, they are easy to find at local craft stores, bead shops, and gem and jewelry shows. Almost any beads can be loaded on the thin 28 gauge wire, even seed beads with tiny holes. Don't overlook existing jewelry pieces. By taking them apart and reusing the old beads, you can create an entirely new look. The number of beads you will need is determined by gauge or number of stitches per inch. When you determine the size stitch you want for the look you are trying to achieve, count how many stitches there are per inch by making a practice piece of crochet wire. Multiply by length and number of rows. As an example, a bracelet with 4 stitches per inch, 7" long, and 5 rows wide would require 140 beads, if you were adding a bead to every stitch.

When working end to end on a bracelet, add about 10% to the length of your first chain row, since working in rows tends to make the "wire fabric" shrink a bit.

It is best to load more beads onto the wire than you think you will need; you can pull off any leftovers after you have cut the wire. If you find you haven't loaded enough beads on your spool, just pull a long length of wire from the spool (enough to finish the project), cut the wire, then load the required beads onto the cut end of the wire. Twist the wire end a few times or tie in a knot to keep the beads from sliding off. Proceed with the final portion of your project and finish off.

If available, it is easier to load beads that are already on a hank or strand of string. Just run the wire into the holes alongside the string for a few inches of beads and then slide out the string onto the wire. When loading loose beads, place in the palm of your hand, a shallow bowl, a paper plate or lay on a towel to keep them from rolling around when you load them onto the wire.

When crocheting with beads, slide a bead from the spool close to the back of the project before starting a stitch with a "yarn over" or "yarn under" wrap around hook. This will trap the bead onto the back of the project which will ultimately be the front or face of your finished piece, unless you are using a large hook and loose stitches where the beads will fall randomly. Any beads that may fall to the other side can be manipulated and poked back into the position you want. It is easier to wrap the wire "yarn under" as the wire is less likely to slip off the hook when pulling the loop through except when making the first chain row which is easier to work "yarn over". Do what feels most comfortable, and you will surely have fun making beautiful necklaces, bracelets, belts, pins, and more.

stitch basics

Loading Beads

1. If you purchase your beads on a strand, you can transfer them directly onto the wire by sliding the straightened end of the wire through several inches of beads then sliding the beads down the wire. Repeat with entire strand adding as many beads as needed for the project.

Making Beaded Chains

2. Use your favorite method to make a slip knot near the end of the loaded wire.

3. The hook should be able to move loosely through the tightened slip knot.

4. For the first beaded chain stitch, slide a bead close to the hook, wrap wire around the hook in a "yarn over" fashion, and pull wire through the slip knot loop.

5. Drop a bead onto every stitch and continue making chains to desired length for first row.

Single Crochet Rows

6. To start the second row, put hook through one loop of previous stitch. Slide a bead close to the hook and work wire "yarn under" hook to begin a single crochet stitch. Pull the wire through the first loop.

7. Wrap wire "yarn under" again and pull through both loops on hook. Continue adding more single crochet stitches until you complete the row.

8. Turn, then add an extra "yarn over" chain stitch (turning chain) without a bead. This will keep your "wire fabric" square with the correct number of stitches in the next row.

9. Make a third row by working back into the last bead stitch of the second row and hooking through two loops of the stitch.

10. Continue adding more single crochet stitches to complete row 3 then repeat for subsequent rows.

11. When you have completed the desired number of rows to create the width you want for your project (four rows shown), cut the wire, leaving an 8" tail, and pull the end through the last loop to tie it off.

Finishing

12. To hide the wire and secure the end, run wire back through a few beads. Cut wire or use to attach clasp.

13. Add clasp by wrapping wire several times around clasp ring then run the end through a few beads before cutting off excess wire.

14. To add the second part of the clasp, attach an 8" piece of wire to the other end of the bracelet or necklace and twist a few times.

15. Wrap wire several times around clasp ring, run end through a few beads, and cut off excess wire.

16. The finished bracelet should fit comfortably around the wrist.

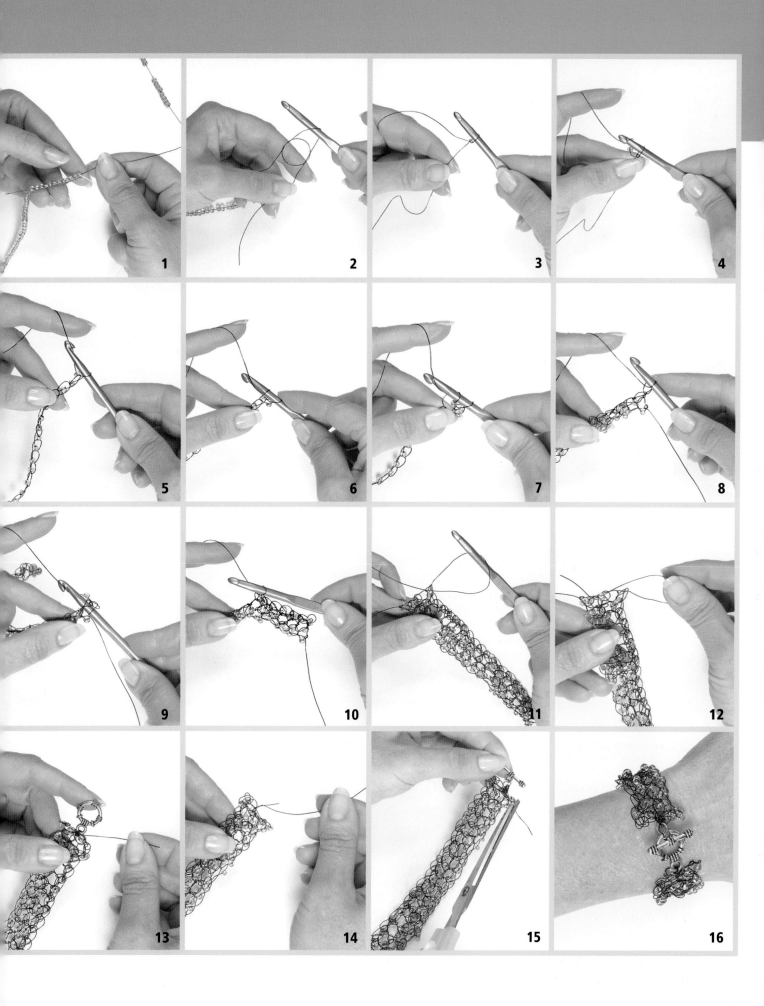

making flowers

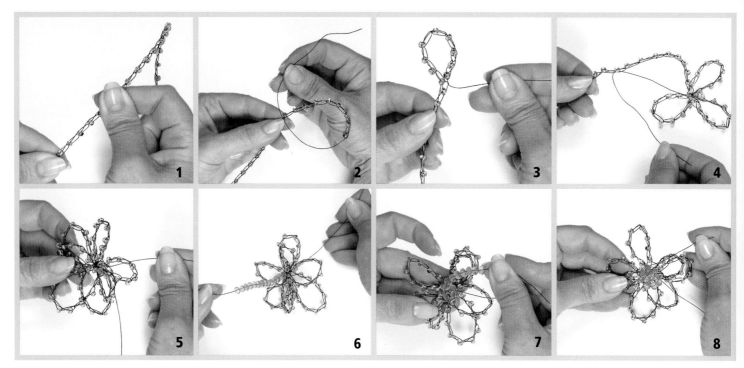

*Use this basic flower construction for
projects on pages 17, 23, 24, 28, and 34.*

1. Determine how many beads you want per loop (petal) and multiply times the number of petals. For instance, nine beads per petal times five petals would be 45 beads total. Load the wire spool with the correct number of beads. Chain a strand using a size D/3.25mm crochet hook, adding a bead to every stitch until all beads are used. End the strand, leaving a 6" or longer tail. Pull tight to stretch out the strand.

2. Starting at the end of the strand, count the number of single chains needed for the first petal and run the wire end through the single chain at this point to make the first petal.

3. Pull tight to close the loop. This intersection will be the center of the flower.

4. Repeat for all the petals, running the wire through the same intersection until reaching the end of the strand.

5. Pull wire tight and thread the wire end in and out of the center a few times to secure it. If desired, you may add another flower made with only chained wire (without beads), using the same method. Attach to the back of the beaded flower and wire together.

6. Make a center for the flower by adding about 2" of larger, contrasting beads to the wire end.

7. Wrap beads around in a circle a few times to make a knot-shaped center.

8. Thread the wire end through the top of the center beads a few times to secure the knot shape. Wire the finished flower to a project or ribbon rosette.

circular tubes

1. Load the appropriate number of beads onto the wire spool. Use a size B/2.55mm steel crochet hook (or hook specified for project) and chain five stitches, adding a bead to every stitch.

2. Place hook back through loop of first stitch and join with a single crochet stitch to make a circle of four stitches.

3. Begin single crocheting in the round, using a "yarn over" stitch.

4. To help maintain the circular shape, insert a cord or heavy shoelace through the center of the circle.

5. Continue working single crochet stitches in the round.

6. You will start to see a spiral pattern after an inch or so of stitching. Continue to work in the round until you have reached the desired length.

7. Cut the wire, leaving a 6" tail, and pull out the last loop to secure the wire.

8. Remove the shoelace and finish project with a clasp or as desired.

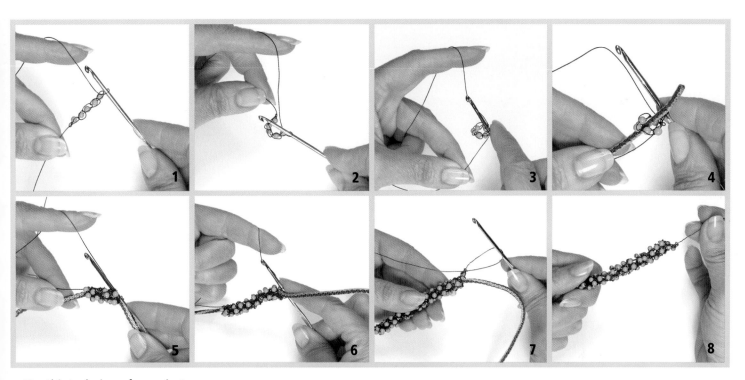

Use this technique for projects on pages 17 and 35.

Materials

28 gauge black wire
Size G/4.00mm metal crochet hook
500 blue and clear beads in various sizes and shapes
8 head pins, 2" long
Large silver toggle clasp
2 large silver cones
3 silver jump rings

Instructions

Load the beads onto the wire spool in random order. Using the basic crochet chain stitch, create five 23" long strands, leaving about 3" of wire at each end for finishing. Add a single medium-to-large bead or up to three small beads in each chain stitch. Chain two more 23" strands without beads. Twist the wire ends together at one end. Separate the seven strands into three sections of 2–2–3 strands and very loosely braid the strands together. Twist together the wires at the other end. Use a head pin to finish each end of the braid. Fold over the head end about ½" and wrap the black wires several times around the fold; snip off excess wire. Pinch the head pin closed to anchor the braid ends. Pull the opposite end of the pin through the silver cone, hiding the braid ends inside the cone. Pull the end of the head pin tight and trim off, leaving ½" of wire. Form into a round loop with pliers, add a jump ring to each loop, and attach a toggle clasp.

For the tassel addition, load five head pins with beads (see photo for bead placement). Make a loop at the end of each pin. Load another head pin with a medium flat bead, a large bead, and another medium flat bead. Cut off the head of the pin and make a loop at each end. Add the five beaded pins to one of the loops and tighten to secure; attach the tassel to a jump ring then to the end of the toggle clasp.

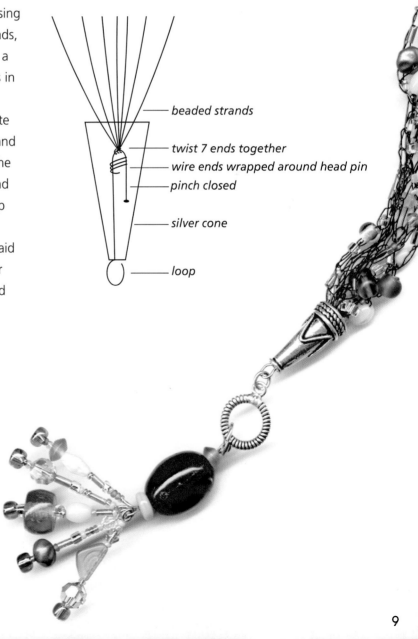

beaded strands

twist 7 ends together
wire ends wrapped around head pin
pinch closed

silver cone

loop

random crystal bracelet

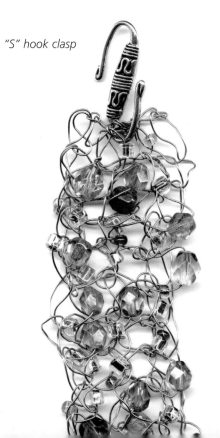

"S" hook clasp

Materials

24 gauge silver wire
Size G/4.00mm metal crochet hook
90 crystal beads in various sizes and colors
Double hook clasp

Instructions

Load the crystal beads onto the wire spool. Crochet a chain 7" long, adding a bead to each stitch (see pages 4-5). Single crochet four rows, adding a bead to every stitch (see pages 4-5). After the last stitch, cut the wire, leaving a 3" tail. Thread tail back through a bead or two and hide inside a bead. Trim excess wire. Attach an "S" hook clasp at one end and hook to the other end of the bracelet to secure.

Materials

28 gauge red wire

28 gauge silver wire

Size B/2.55mm steel crochet hook

300 pink/silver 3mm beads

51 clear 6mm crystal faceted beads

1" decorative button with shank for clasp

Instructions

Load all pink beads onto the red wire spool. Crochet chain for 5½", adding a bead to every other stitch. Single crochet another nine rows for a total of ten crocheted rows. Load 51 clear crystal faceted beads onto the silver wire spool. Starting on one long side, use silver wire to single crochet a row around three sides, adding a bead to each stitch to create an edging to the bracelet. Make a 1¾" chain loop for the clasp. Center it on the fourth side and wire to the bracelet, leaving ½" between ends. Use wire to attach a 1" button to the opposite side of the bracelet. Slip the loop over the button to secure the clasp.

red wire bracelet

Materials

26 gauge silver wire

Size D/3.25mm crochet hook

3mm mirrored pink and silver seed beads
    25 pink, 25 silver

16 pink and white 5mm or 6mm natural shaped pearls

1 smoky 6mm faceted crystal bead

1 white 4mm round pearl bead

1 pink ⅝" long briolette bead

Instructions

Load the seed beads and pearls onto the wire randomly.
Make five chain stitches, adding a bead to every stitch.
Connect to the first stitch to make a circle. Single crochet
in the round, adding a bead to every stitch and adding an
extra stitch (two stitches in one hole) every other stitch.
This will make the circle larger and enable you to form it
into a dome shape as you work. Stitch in the round until
the circle is 1½" in diameter. End the wire, leaving a 10"
tail. Fold the tail in half and twist the wire into a double
thick wire "rope." Shape into a loop that is ⅜" in diameter
for the pendant hanger. Wrap the end around the base of
the loop three times and snip off the end. Crimp the end
of the wire with pliers to hide it.

Make the drop bead by attaching an 8" piece of wire to
the bottom of the pendant. Run the wire through the
smoky crystal bead, small pearl bead, and the briolette
then back through the pearl and smoky bead. Pull the wire
tight, secure it at the bottom of the pendant, and hide the
end in the crocheted stitches. Hang this pendant from a silver choker, heavy chain, or ribbon.

Materials

28 gauge copper wire

Size B/2.55mm steel crochet hook

16" strand or 327 pale green 3mm beads

Five 8mm matching briolettes

Toggle clasp

Instructions

Crochet a 14" long chain, adding one bead to each stitch. Refer to diagram for pattern of necklace. Single crochet the second row back 3½" without adding beads. Make a chain of seven stitches with a bead on each stitch. Count four beaded stitches from the 3½" mark and reattach to main chain, using a single crochet stitch. This creates a V-shaped loop if you pull the middle bead down tight. Repeat eight times for a total of nine loops. Finish off the rest of the main chain with just wire and single crochet stitches until you reach the starting point. Make a new slip knot and chain seven stitches with a bead on each stitch. Attach and hide wire at the bottom "V" bead on the first loop. After the seventh stitch, single crochet a stitch to the next "V" point on the next loop and repeat seven times

for a total of eight loops on the second row. End and hide the wire. Make a new slip knot and single crochet five stitches, adding a bead to each stitch. Attach this wire to the bottom "V" bead on the first loop and hide the wire end. After the fifth stitch single crochet onto the next "V" point and repeat for a total of seven five-bead loops on the third row. For the fourth row of loops, skip the first loop and attach the wire end to the second loop. Make a five bead loop and repeat for a total of four loops. End and hide the wire. Add a last center loop of five beads between the second and third loops of the fourth row to create a center point at the middle of the necklace.

Add briolettes and small beads to the bottom points of the five "V" loops at the bottom of the necklace. Add small beads in a 2-4-6-4-2 sequence with the six beads on the center loop to create the longest drop bead. Twist the wire ends around the top of the drop section and cut and pinch the ends with pliers to hide them. Add a toggle clasp to the necklace ends. Manipulate the wire to give the necklace a pretty and graceful shape to be worn as a choker.

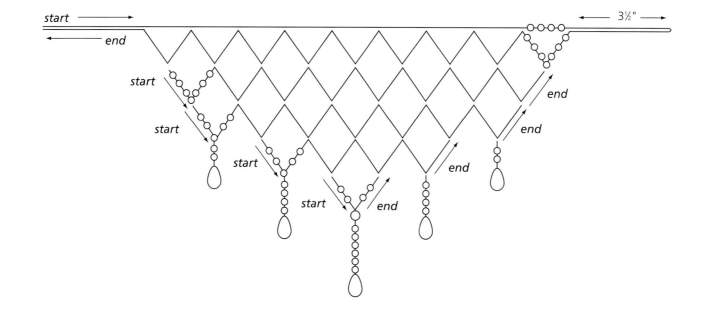

Materials

28 gauge navy blue wire
Blue micro fiber cotton crochet yarn
H/5.00mm aluminum crochet hook
B/2.55mm steel crochet hook
Large needle
Iridescent blue 3mm beads
5 medium crystal faceted beads between
    7mm and 12mm

Instructions

Using just the blue cotton yarn and size H crochet hook, double crochet two 4" squares (see diagrams). Use the same yarn and a large needle to sew three sides together. To make the purse strap, first load 200 blue beads onto the cotton yarn, using a thin wire to make a threading needle (see diagrams below). Using a size H crochet hook, chain four stitches, adding a bead to each stitch, then make a circle by stitching back into the first stitch. Single crochet in a continuous circle, adding a bead to each stitch until your strap is 12" long. Fasten off. Use yarn to sew the strap ends to the inside of the purse at the top corners. Load approximately 256 iridescent blue beads on the navy blue wire spool. Make five flowers of various sizes using size B crochet hook. They should measure between 1½" to 2" in diameter with five to seven petals (see page 6). For each flower make a large crystal bead center, using a small blue bead on top to anchor the large bead. Wire centers to flowers then wire randomly to front of purse.

Double Crochet

Yarn over, insert hook, yarn over and pull through one loop, yarn over and pull through two loops, yarn over and pull through remaining two loops.

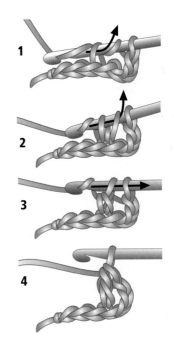

Loading Beads on Yarn

Cut a piece of wire 5" long and fold in half over the crochet yarn about 2" from the end. Trim ends of wire to even out and pinch "eye" end to secure the yarn (A). Thread beads on wire needle (B) and slide down onto yarn (C).

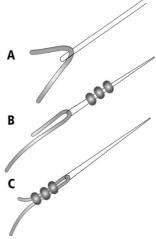

citrine necklace

Materials

28 gauge gold wire
Size H/5.00mm metal crochet hook
180 small citrine nugget beads
9 amber 7mm round faceted crystal beads
1 citrine 12mm round faceted bead
Gold round clasp

Instructions

Load 120 small citrine nuggets onto the wire spool. Chain a 15" strand, adding a bead to each stitch. Treble crochet along the entire chain (see diagrams), adding one bead to the top before starting another treble stitch. Make loose stitches for a lacy look. End the wire and add a gold clasp to each end.

Make the flower medallion by following the pattern provided. Load nine 7mm beads on the wire and join into a circle. Thread a large round bead on the tail, position it in the center of the circle, and secure by wrapping the wire end between beads. Load 36 small citrine nugget beads on the wire spool. Adding a bead to every stitch, single crochet between two of the 7mm beads then add three chain stitches before reattaching with a single crochet stitch between the next two beads. Stitch all the way around the ring of beads. End the wire and attach the flower medallion to the center of the choker.

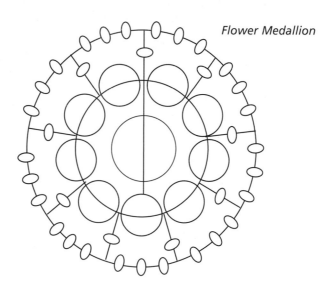

Flower Medallion

Treble Crochet

Yarn over twice, insert hook in stitch 4th chain from hook (then every chain thereafter). YO and pull up a loop (4 loops on hook) (fig. 1), (YO and draw through 2 loops on hook) 3 times (figs. 2-4).

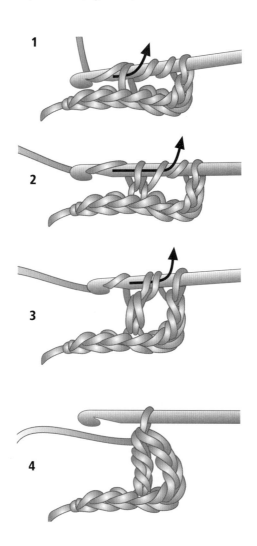

1

2

3

4

Materials

28 gauge green wire

28 gauge gold wire

Size G/4.00mm metal crochet hook

82 pink 4mm crystal faceted beads

2 gold 5mm crystal faceted beads

2 pink 6mm crystal faceted beads

Assorted beads for butterfly body and wings

Large opalescent briolette bead for butterfly head

9mm metallic polyester thread in blue, green, and red

Black, pink, and red 5mm pony beads for fringe trim

Instructions

Load the gold wire spool with one 6mm pink bead, one 5mm gold bead, and eighty two 4mm pink beads. Add a 5mm gold bead and a 6mm pink bead. Crochet a chain, adding a bead to every stitch, until it measures 32" long for the strap of the purse.

Using the green wire, make a chain of 36 stitches. Single crochet back into the first stitch to join into a circle then stitch in the round until you have a tube shape that is 3" deep. End the wire and press the tube flat to make a 2½" x 3" rectangular shape. Use more green wire to slip stitch the bottom of the bag closed. Wire the handle to the top corners. Cut an 8" long strand of blue, green, and red metallic threads for each fringe piece. Fold in half, hook folded ends around hook, and pull through bottom of bag, starting at one side. Insert strand ends into loop pulled through and pull gently to tighten. Repeat seven times along bottom of bag. Knot on randomly the black, pink, and red pony beads (see photo). Make the butterfly with gold wire, following the diagram above, and secure with wire to the top center area of purse.

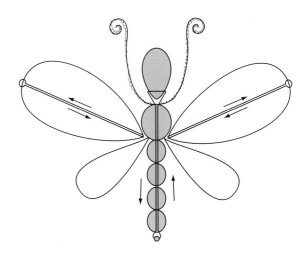

Making the Butterfly

1. Make body of butterfly by wiring a white briolette with pink faceted beads and running wire back to body intersection below large bead.

2. Make wings by attaching 12" of wire to body section and loading pink and red beads onto wire. Make two large loops and two small loops, wrapping the wire around the body after each loop.

3. Add the center beads to each large loop by starting at the main intersection below the large bead and loading 1" of red and black beads onto the wire. Wrap wire around center of large loop and reinsert the wire end back through the beads to end at the body. Twist all wire ends together and use to attach to the front of the bag.

4. For the antennas, twist two 3" pieces of wire together to make a thicker rope-like wire. Twist around the base of the briolette at the center point of the wire and coil the ends with pliers (see photo).

5. Use another piece of wire to further secure the butterfly body to the purse.

Materials
28 gauge blue wire
28 gauge red wire
Size D/3.25mm crochet hook
Multicolored seed beads
Five 2" head pins
Assorted crystal faceted beads up to 6mm

Instructions
For the purse strap, load 130 multicolored seed beads onto the blue wire spool in random order. Crochet chain stitches until all beads are used, making a strand approximately 26" long.

For the body of the purse, crochet 3" of chain stitches with the blue wire then join into a circle by working back into the first stitch. Start double crochet stitches (see page 17), working in the round until you have a tubular shape that is 2" deep. End the wire, flatten the tube, and sew the bottom edge closed with blue wire. Wire the strap to the top two corners of the purse, incorporating wire ends into the body. Create a small flower with red wire by making a 7" long strand of chains then forming a petal every inch for a total of 7 petals (see page 6). Add a 6mm pink crystal bead for the center. Wire the flower to the top left corner of the purse. Make dangling fringe for the bottom of the purse by loading five head pins with beads as shown in the photo. Cut each pin, leaving ¼" at end for loop. Use pliers to form a small loop. Hook loops of head pins through purse wire, spacing pins out evenly along purse bottom then close loops to secure.

coral pocket

Materials
28 gauge red wire
Size B/2.55mm crochet hook
Spiky coral beads
Turquoise seed beads
5mm turquoise beads
7mm silver bead
Small piece black felt (bag back)
Needle and black thread

Instructions
Load red wire randomly with approximately 250 coral and turquoise beads, ending with 14 coral beads. Chain 14 stitches, adding a coral bead each stitch for about 2¼". Single crochet next rows adding a bead to every stitch until completing a 3½"x 2¼" solidly beaded rectangle (see pages 4-5). Cut a piece of black felt the same size. Place the beaded rectangle on top. Use black thread to sew the two together on three edges, leaving open the top edge with the coral beads. To make the strap, chain two 25" long strands of red wire without beads. Load 130 turquoise seed beads onto the red wire spool and chain a third 25" long strand, adding a bead to every stitch. Twist the three strands together at one end, braid to the other end, then twist together to hold the braid in place. Add a 5mm turquoise bead to each end and secure the ends to the top corners of the bag. Make the bottom beaded fringe, using a 3' long piece of red wire. Attach the wire to the right bottom corner of the bag. Add a 5mm turquoise bead (one of 14) then make a ½" long loop. Twist the wire around itself at the start of the loop to secure it. Holding the bead at the other end of the loop, continue twisting the wire until the bead rests snugly at the end of the twisted loop. To add more fringe, lace the wire through the next bottom stitch as if sewing with the wire. Make a loop, add another bead, and finish as before. Repeat all along the bottom of the bag. Make a five-petal flower, using red wire and 5mm turquoise beads (5 per petal) with a silver bead center (see page 6 for flower basics). Attach to the top right corner of the bag.

Materials

28 gauge black wire

Size G/4.00mm crochet hook

26 magnetic hematite beads

52 blue 4mm seed beads

50 aqua 4mm square-cut beads

25 light blue 4mm faceted crystal beads

2 blue 8mm faceted crystal beads

Instructions

Load the black wire spool with a hematite bead, blue bead, aqua bead, blue faceted crystal bead, aqua bead, and blue bead. Repeat 24 times for a total of 25 sets of beads and end with a hematite bead. Crochet a chain, adding a bead to each stitch until all beads are used and the strand measures approximately 48" long. Give a little tug to the chain to tighten the beads and make the chain thinner. Add an 8mm blue faceted crystal bead and a 4mm blue seed bead to each wire end and run the end wire back up through the two beads; wrap and snip off the ends. This chain can be worn as a bracelet, anklet, choker, necklace, or lariat as the magnets hold together at 2" intervals and can be wrapped around as desired.

variation

Materials

26 gauge silver wire

17 magnetic hematite beads

34 blue 4mm seed beads

32 silver ½" bugle beads

32 blue/purple 4mm faceted crystal beads

32 aqua 4mm square-cut beads

16 clear 6mm faceted crystal beads

2 clear 6mm teardrop faceted crystal beads

This is a variation on the project at left and is not crocheted, but instead strung on wire for a closer fit when wrapped around itself. String the beads as shown in the photo below. Finish the ends by adding a clear teardrop bead and a 4mm blue bead. Run the wire ends back through the beads then wrap the wire around itself a few times; trim ends. This design makes a great party favor for guests. Display at your party table as a napkin ring with a small tag, and your delighted guests can wear their gifts home.

*Versatile Magnets shown as a partially wrapped bracelet (left).
Variation shown as a wrapped anklet (right).*

Materials

28 gauge wire in desired colors

Size B/2.55 metal crochet hook

3mm or 4mm seed beads in coordinating colors

Large beads for flower centers

14" satin wired ribbon, 1½" to 2" wide

Needle and thread

1" metal pin back

Green Ribbon Pin

Gather 14" of 1½" wide green wired ribbon into a rosette, as shown in the diagram. Make a wire and bead flower by first loading amber, green, pink, and gold seed beads onto the gold wire spool (refer to directions on page 6). Chain 20", adding a bead to every stitch. For the petals gather up lengths of the chain between 1½" to 3", making 10 loops of various sizes to form the flower. Load sixteen 6mm beads in matching colors onto the wire and make a knotted center for the flower, following steps 6-8 on page 6. Center the beaded flower on the rosette. Using needle and thread, sew a pin back to the back of the rosette, catching the center of the flower as you sew.

Fuchsia Ribbon Pin

Gather 14" of 1½" wide peachy/fuchsia variegated, wired ribbon into a rosette, as shown in the diagram. Make a wire and bead flower by first loading 4mm green seed beads onto green wire (refer to directions on page 6). For the top petal layer, chain 12", adding a bead to every stitch then gather the chain into six 2" loops. For the bottom petal layer, chain 12½", using only wire, and gather into five 2½" loops. Wire the two layers together with the beaded layer on top, twisting the wire ends together on the back. Make a flower center, following steps 6-8 on page 6. Load fifty 4mm green seed beads onto the wire spool and create a large knot by wrapping the wire around four times. Center the beaded flower on the rosette. Using needle and thread, sew a pin back to the back of the rosette, catching the center of the flower as you sew.

Purple and Pink Ribbon Pin

Gather 14" of 2" wide pink wired ribbon into a rosette as shown in the diagram. Make an additional ribbon rosette, using 1½" wide purple wired ribbon. Layer on top of pink rosette then sew both together at the center, using needle and thread. Make a wire and bead flower by first loading purple wire with forty five 3mm round garnet beads (refer to directions on page 6). Crochet a chain, adding a bead to every stitch, until all beads are used. For the top petal layer, make five loops with nine beads each and gather into a flower. Make an additional petal layer using only wire; chain 18" and gather into six loops. Make a flower center, following steps 6-8 on page 6. Load the wire spool with five 7mm pink faceted crystal beads, alternating with five 4mm clear faceted crystal beads. Wrap twice to make a knot shape and secure to flower center. End wire and trim. Center the beaded flower on the rosette. Using needle and thread, sew a pin back to the back of the rosette, catching the center of the flower as you sew.

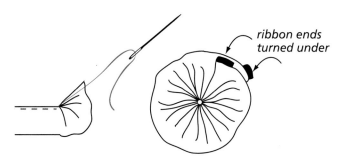

ribbon ends turned under

Stitch gathering thread close to ribbon edge. Pull thread tight to gather into circle. Fold back raw edges.

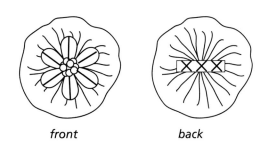

front   *back*

Sew on pin back using needle and thread.

daisy belt

Materials

18 gauge black wire

28 gauge black wire

28 gauge copper wire

Size G/4.00mm crochet hook

Size B/2.55mm crochet hook

140 red seed beads

4mm light blue faceted crystal beads

6mm light blue faceted crystal beads

7 blue 7mm iridescent beads

2 blue 10mm faceted crystal beads

1 peach 14mm faceted crystal bead

1 blue seed bead

Instructions

Bend the heavy 18 gauge black wire into a five-petal flower using needle nose pliers and wrapping the wire around the center after each loop. Cut wire, leaving a 1" tail to make a hook for attaching the belt. Bend back ⅛" on the end and squeeze tight with pliers to round off the end of the wire. Now bend the wire over so it is parallel with the back of the flower to complete the hook. Load the red seed beads onto the copper wire spool. Using the size B crochet hook, add a row of slip stitches with a bead on each stitch all around the wire petal. Slip stitch around the petal with wire in back. Insert hook into wire petal from front to back, wire over then pull wire back through petal and slip through loop on hook. Bring wire over hook and slip through loop on hook. Repeat working your way around the wire petal.

Complete all five petals and cut the wire. Load approximately 75 light blue 4mm beads onto the copper wire spool. Starting at the flower center, wrap the wire around each petal, filling in the empty center with the blue beads. The beads should be closely packed, and you will need to wrap about 7 times to fill in a petal with about 15 beads. The red seed beads will help space apart the rows of blue beads, so they won't slip together. Start with a row of one or two beads at the petal bottom then use three to four beads at the widest part of the petal. When you reach the top of the petal, wrap back toward the center using just wire. This provides extra support for the beads. After filling in all five petals, wrap the wire around the flower center a few times to secure and cut. Add a flower center using six 7mm blue iridescent beads and a 10mm round blue bead, referring to steps 6-8 on page 6. Wrap the 7mm beads around the 10mm blue bead.

To make the chain belt, use a size G crochet hook and 28 gauge black wire. Load the wire with a 6mm blue bead then ten 4mm blue beads. Repeat five more times and end with a 6mm blue bead. Leaving a 3" tail, chain 18 stitches then begin adding a bead every other stitch until the last segment of ten 4mm blue beads. At this point add a bead to every stitch until all beads are used. Cut the wire, leaving an 8" tail. Add larger beads on the end to provide extra weight. Load in the following order: 7mm blue iridescent bead, 10mm round faceted crystal, 4mm light blue faceted crystal, 14mm peach round faceted crystal, 4mm light blue faceted crystal (see photo). Add a tiny blue seed bead at the end and run the wire back up through the larger beads. Wrap the wire end around itself and snip off. Attach the chained belt to the back of the flower by wrapping the starting tail around the hook at the flower center.

southwest belt

Materials

28 gauge silver wire

Size G/4.00mm crochet hook

140 turquoise 3mm round beads

130 red coral 4mm round beads

140 red coral spiky beads

Tassels:

   16 medium silver beads

   16 small silver beads

   2 large silver beads (approximately ⅝")

   Black leather cording

Two silver jump rings

8 assorted large turquoise beads

Instructions

Load 3mm turquoise beads onto silver wire and chain a 50" long strand, adding a bead to every stitch. Do the same with the round coral beads and also with the spiky coral beads. Crochet three more 50" strands without adding beads. Twist all six strands together tightly at one end and divide into three pairs with a wire chain and beaded chain in each pair. Braid strands together then secure end by twisting tightly. The braid will be about 46" long.

Finish both ends in the same manner. Twist tightly for about 2". Measure ¾" past the last chain stitch and fold the wire back. Wrap around itself a few times to make a loop. Cut off excess wire. Poke the loop through the hole of the large silver bead. Use a large needle or the end of needle nose pliers to open the loop, enlarging it so it won't slip back through the hole in the bead. Attach a silver jump ring to the loop. Cut four 6" lengths of leather cording. Tie these to the jump ring, using an overhand

knot. Embellish the cord ends with small and medium silver beads and four turquoise beads. Vary the size and placement of the silver beads and incorporate two turquoise beads on each side of the knot. Tie off each cord end in an overhand knot to secure the beads. After completing both belt ends, trim leather cords, leaving about ½" below each knot.

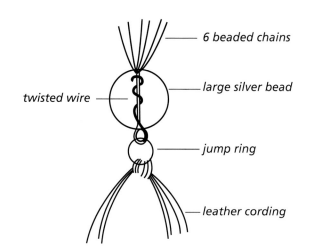

6 beaded chains

large silver bead

twisted wire

jump ring

leather cording

following the directions on page 6. For the bottom layer of petals, chain a 36" long strand and divide into nine loops. For the top layer of petals, load 100 turquoise beads on the wire. Chain a 15" long strand, adding a bead to each stitch, then divide into five loops that are slightly smaller than the loops on the bottom layer. Cut a 15" length of wire and use one end to wire the two petal layers together at the flower center (beaded petals on top). Load 50 turquoise beads on the free end. Beginning at the center, spiral beads around three times in a circle then thread the end back through the flower center and secure on the back. Use ends to wire the entire flower to center of necklace. This necklace can also be worn as a bracelet by wrapping around the wrist three times.

Finishing

1. Fold the twisted end in half, leaving twice enough wire to accommodate your finishing bead or cone plus a small loop. Twist once around the wire to secure and make a loop. Use pliers to pinch the loop nearly flat to fit through the barrel bead.

2. Thread the wire through the barrel bead, leaving the folded end exposed. Use a large needle or awl to open the folded end into a loop.

3. Finish by adding a jump ring and clasp of your choice.

Materials

28 gauge black wire
Size H/5mm metal crochet hook
Size B/2.55mm metal crochet hook
Turquoise seed beads
2 silver barrel beads
Silver toggle clasp

Instructions

Load approximately 120 turquoise seed beads onto the black wire spool. Using the size H crochet hook, chain three 22" long strands, adding a bead to every other stitch. Twist the three wire ends together and braid the strands to the end, making sure the braid lies flat. The braiding will shrink the length of the necklace to about 20". Secure the braiding by twisting the three wire ends together, then continue twisting to make a single wire,. Twist the other end, of the braid into a single wire also. Finish by adding a barrel bead to each end, followed by a silver toggle clasp (see finishing steps 1–3). Crochet a large double-layered flower, using the size B crochet hook and

multicolored bracelet

Materials

28 gauge green wire
Size B/2.55mm steel crochet hook
3mm lined Rochaille beads in six colors
Small silver toggle clasp

Instructions

Load approximately 120 beads in random colors onto the green wire. Make five chain stitches, adding a bead to each stitch. Join the beaded chain into a circle by connecting the first and fifth stitches together with a single crochet stitch (see pages 4-5). This will leave you with four stitches to begin your circular tube (see page 7). Continue single crocheting in the round, adding a bead to each stitch until the "rope" measures 7" or as long as desired for bracelet. Cut wire, leaving a 6" tail. Add silver toggle clasp to ends of bracelet and trim excess wire.

resources

Most supplies used to create the designs in this book are available at your local craft retailer. For specialty beads or further assistance, consult the companies below.

Rings & Things (ColourCraft© Wire, beads, and findings)

304 E. 2nd Avenue

P.O. Box 450

Spokane, WA 99210-0450

509-624-8565

www.rings-things.com

Soft Flex Company (beads, Artistic Wire)

P.O. Box 80

Sonoma, CA 95476

707-938-3539

www.softflexcompany.com

Rio Grande (beads, sterling silver wire, and findings)

7500 Bluewater Rd. NW

Albuquerque, NM 87121-1962

800-545-6566

www.riogrande.com

Mode Int'l, Inc. (beads)

1572 61st Street

Brooklyn, NY 11219

718-259-9224

www.modebeads.com

Produced By:
Kooler Design Studio • 399 Taylor Blvd., Ste. 104, Pleasant Hill, CA 94523 • www.koolerdesign.com
Creative Director, Donna Kooler • Editor-in-Chief, Judy Swager
Writer, Book Designer, and Photo Stylist, Basha Kooler
Production and Graphic Artist, María Rodríguez •
Proofreader, Char Randolph • Editorial Assistant, McKenzie Mortensen
Photographer, Dianne Woods • Model, Ana Kischmischian